The Natural Science of Money – Primer

By Joseph Thomas Plummer

Loaves and Fishes

This is not
the age of information.

This is NOT
the age of information.

Forget the news,
and the radio,
and the blurred screen.

This is the time
of loaves
and fishes.

*People are hungry
and one good word is bread
for a thousand.*

-- David Whyte

Under the microscope.

"Why should we, however, in economics, have to plead ignorance of the sort of facts on which, in the case of a physical theory, a scientist would certainly be expected to give precise information?"

-Friedrich August von Hayek

The idea of trickle-down economics is a metaphor rooted in a misunderstanding of the concept of gravity. The basic idea behind trickle-down economics is that if you make the rich better off, then they will make the whole population better off in a process that resembles water trickling from the top of a tree down to its roots. This is a nice thought. However, water trickles from the top of a tree down to its roots because of a gravitational force. The flow of money also adheres to the theory of gravity. More precisely, money adheres to the laws of nature and can be described and better understood using the natural sciences.

The field of economics uses the same language used in the natural sciences- mathematics. So it is no surprise that the words used to describe the mathematics are also similar. Boom, bust, crash, momentum, the velocity of money, the rate of exchange, growth, decline, flow, surge. These words are as useful in describing an economic event as they are in describing a physical event or an event in nature. If we are using the same words and the same mathematics that we use in the natural sciences to describe economics, then is it possible that the natural laws, theories, and constructs that we have discovered and developed might also be useful in the study and practice of economics and related disciplines?

The purpose of this document is to explore through metaphors, analogies, and anecdotes the potentially significant intersection of economics and the natural sciences. This intersection undoubtedly exists, but the depth, relevance, and value of this intersection is unclear. And, while we are using metaphors, analogies, and anecdotes as a means of exploration, our end goal is to test and potentially reinvent the fundamentals of economics. The "first principles" of economics are now under the microscope.

Units matter.

"A careful analysis of the process of observation in atomic physics has shown that the subatomic particles have no meaning as isolated entities, but can only be understood as interconnections between the preparation of an experiment and the subsequent measurement."

-Erwin Schrodinger

In economics, as in any science, the units of measurement are vital to understanding outcomes. To measure the value of anything in an economy, we use dollars as our unit. To be more precise, we use fractions of dollars. If we are discussing the budget for NASA, it is described as less than one cent of every tax dollar. We don't think about cents very often anymore. They are generally overlooked in purchasing decisions. However, understanding the level of granularity in our money is very useful in developing good public finance practices. Furthermore, it is important to understand how small money can be. For example, if our money supply is $100, and our minimum unit of currency is $1, then it will be difficult to be precise and just in our transactions and in our taxation.

Luckily, we have a very small minimum unit of currency (the penny). This allows us to be very precise in our transactions and taxation. We don't really have to worry about day-to-day economic injustice. In general, if I pay $5.50 for something, I am getting $5.50 of value. In the previous case where the minimum unit of currency is $1, I would have either paid $5 or $6. Either way, this would've been a deadweight loss of value to the economy and a miniature injustice.

Using our small minimum unit of currency, we can also address issues like deteriorating infrastructure and collapsing ecosystems without breaking our budget. Let's say we had a rough winter and poured tons upon tons of salt on the roads. As a result, in the spring we have a record number of potholes and a record increase in harmful runoff. The government can impose very small taxes that raise the appropriate amount of funds for infrastructure and environmental maintenance, while not effecting purchasing decisions. This is doable up to a certain threshold where the cost of maintaining or rehabilitating exceeds the revenue generated by small insignificant increases to tax rates. At this point, the government generally does one of three things- 1) ignore the infrastructure and environmental problems, 2) go into debt to pay for the infrastructure and environmental problems, or 3) use money from other budgets like education, welfare, and defense. There is a fourth option at the federal level- increasing the money supply.

When we analyze economics at the individual level, it is difficult to develop a usable scientific theory. However, if we observe and analyze the relationships between individuals, the relationships between individuals and organizations, and the relationships between individuals and their governments, then the development of usable scientific theories is possible. It is only through understanding the interconnectedness of the system of systems that make up our economy that we will be able to advance the science of economics. While it is not possible to develop the science of economics by looking only at the decisions of the individual, it is also not possible to develop the science of economics without considering the decisions of the individual. Individuals have no meaning as isolated entities just as a penny on the ground has virtually no value. But we need the individual, and we need the penny for our economy to work.

The Physics of Money

"Physics and philosophy are at most a few thousand years old, but probably have lives of thousands of millions of years stretching in front of them."

-Sir James Jeans

There is a significant intersection between physics and economics that has not been thoroughly explored. The velocity of money is just one very basic illustration of this intersection. We can go deep into the field of physics to find theories that are useful in the development of economics as a science. The question we need to ask as we explore is this, "Is this theory a metaphor for a concept in economics or can this theory be directly applied to economics?" In the case of the velocity of money, our understanding of velocity in physics is pretty much the same as our understanding of velocity in economics. So, we can say that velocity is not a metaphor, but a direct application. It is simply the rate of movement in both physics and economics.

As was previously stated, the theory of trickle-down economics is based on a misunderstanding of the concept of gravity. Water trickles down from the top of the tree to the roots, because gravity exists. Does gravity also exist in economics? In physics, we represent the gravitational force exerted on an object using the formula $F = G(M_1M_2)/r^2$, where M_1 and M_2 are the masses of two objects, r is the distance between those objects, and G is some gravitational constant. This representation of a gravitational force is certainly useable as a metaphor. The masses can be described as masses of money and the radius can be described as the distance, geographically or in the market, between the two masses of money.

These ideas are useful as both metaphor and potentially direct applications. We can easily consider our understanding in physics of kinetic and potential energy, momentum, thermodynamics, and properties of fluids. These are the low hanging fruit in this exploration. Take your pick. Kinetic energy is a function of mass and velocity. So, we can attempt to directly apply the concept of kinetic energy to economics. There is some mass of money moving through the economy at some velocity, and we can use these numbers to decide what an economic kinetic energy might be. Likewise, we can directly apply the concept of potential energy to economics. This might be useful for understanding how savings and long-term investments could impact the economy. There is some amount of money (m) being saved by a person. That person is in the middle class, which we can use to derive some "height" (h). And, again there is some gravitational constant. So it follows potential energy (U) is equal to mass (m) multiplied by height (h) multiplied by some gravitational constant (g). $U=mgh$. The height (h) in this application might be too metaphoric, but it makes sense that money in savings in the lower class might have more of an effect on the economy than an equal amount of money in savings in the upper class. Imagine a poor person deciding to spend $100 of savings versus a rich person deciding to spend $100 of savings. Maybe it would have an equal impact on the economy. Maybe it would depend how the $100 is spent. It is reasonable to suggest that a dollar spent by a poor person is likely to have more touch points in the economy than a dollar spent by a rich person.

Imagine the application of momentum to the field of political economics. Consider two opposing political candidates running for public office. Both raise money (m) for their campaigns and spend it at some rate (v). The two similar masses collide with each other at similar velocities. The result? Zero movement. Zero progress in either direction. People talk about political pendulums, which are good illustrations of this. Of course there are other ways to influence political progress that don't involve money.

The deeper we go into the study of physics, the more specific and obscure the metaphors and applications become. We could apply James Jeans' theories relating to expansion and contraction of interstellar clouds to the expansion and contraction of an economy or at a smaller scale a market or industry. We could apply chaos theory to financial forecasting models. We could apply Einstein's theory of relativity to income inequality and labor economics. And, we could apply principles of electricity and magnetism to the economics of development. And it is likely that some of this has already been done, perhaps without drawing attention to the significant overlap of the two disciplines. In any case, the door is open, and now we simply need to encourage more people to walk through it.

The Living Economy

"There are three types of biomimicry – one is copying form and shape, another is copying a process, like photosynthesis in a leaf, and the third is mimicking at an ecosystem's level, like building a nature-inspired city."

-Janine Benyus

Using chemistry to advance the science of economics is a little bit more difficult than using physics. Chemistry looks at what makes up our world. What elements are present in each thing on the planet. At first glance, chemistry doesn't seem very helpful in the context of economics. However, if we consider how nature uses chemistry, we might be able to extract certain strategies on how we might use money. Also, if we consider how we use chemistry to describe and understand the material properties of the world, then we might be able to develop a similar set of tools in economics to describe and understand properties of the economic world.

It is no coincidence that the roots of the words economy and ecosystem are the same. By understanding the natural world better, we can also understand our economy better. We can start with basic comparisons between the forms and structures we see in nature and the forms and structures we see in businesses, industries, and markets. And, the building off that knowledge base we can develop our understanding of organizational and market interactions.

Our economy is a living, breathing thing. Everything in our economy can be described by something in nature. Whether it is a business cycle, a merger, or a bankruptcy, nature has mimicked the same function, and in many cases given us examples of how to create an efficient outcome.

Where we live matters.

"Spirit of place! It is for this we travel, to surprise its subtlety; and where it is a strong and dominant angel, that place, seen once, abides entire in the memory with all its own accidents, its habits, its breath, its name."

-Alice Meynell

Imagine for a moment where you grew up. Maybe you grew up on a farm. Maybe you grew up in the city. Maybe you grew up in the suburbs. Maybe you grew up on a military base. In any case, you grew up in a place. And, that place has characteristics that influence the way an economy can operate. The economics of a farming community might be very different from the economics of an urban community. More specifically, the constraints and societal norms that define the economics of a place will be different. This is the same in the physical world.

There are places that are close to water, places that are high in the mountains, places that are in the desert, places that have seasons, and places that don't. All of these characteristics help us understand how the physical world will operate in that place. Imagine how an athlete might perform on a cold, snowy night in the mountains versus a warm sunny day along the coast with a light breeze. These are two examples that show a clear contrast, but the differences among places could also be very subtle. Imagine a hockey player skating on hard brittle ice versus a hockey player skating on soft wet ice. We consider these differences for the purposes of evaluating an athlete's performance. In the same way, we should consider the characteristics of a place when evaluating a place.

In studying and comparing international economic practices, it is difficult to compare the economy of two countries and determine which one is stronger. It is too easy to simply compare the GDP of countries and determine that the higher GDP is the higher performing economy. A more thorough understanding of the places where economies exist will lead to a more real and useful set of economic best practices.

Theory of Everything.

"I have noticed that even people who claim everything is predestined, and that we can do nothing to change it, look before they cross the road."

- Stephen Hawking

It is easy to understand how our economy started and evolved over time. In the natural sciences, we have been able to gather information about the history of the planet, the evolution of the human race, and even the creation of our universe. In economics, we have been able to document the evolution of the human economy. This is not so difficult. We can easily look back at our economic history and find an initial operating condition.   You need wheat. I have wheat. You have ore. I need ore. I will trade you wheat for ore. Boom (or is it Bang?). A resource economy is born.

As an individual in a prehistoric economy, you are either resource rich or resource poor. This is naturally based entirely on where you are born and to what family or tribe. So, if you are resource poor, this means you need to find new resources, steal resources, or create something valuable to a resource rich person that you can then trade for resources. If you are resource rich, all you need to do is defend your resources and make trades as you deem necessary or desirable. At this point, trading resources for services becomes essential for the resource poor to survive. I don't have any resources, but I will provide you with labor in exchange for some of your resources. Boom. A service economy is born.

This is good. We have people exchanging goods and services. However, we are limited as individuals, communities, and a society based on the supply and demand of the resources in our region. We can of course travel from region to region to make trades, but trading goods for services becomes more difficult if you are planning on returning to your home region. So again, we are limited by the resources available to us. There must be a way to create some sort of medium of exchange so that we are not constrained by the nature of our resources and our region. Enter money.

With the creation of money, we as individuals, communities, and a society are unconstrained by our resources, our skills, and our market. Assuming our money is acceptable everywhere we might travel, we can buy any resource we want with our money. Before money, we would have to find someone that both wanted wheat and had something that we wanted. Before money, the amount of wheat traded for each unit of ore would be completely dependent on the individual we were trading with. Money is a good thing.

This quick and dirty analysis of a hypothetical economic history allows us to think about our monetary system in a very simple and digestible way. Given a large complex international monetary system with many currencies, resources, and regional conditions, it is beneficial to work with a primitive model of an economy and build up from a set of base conditions. Using these base conditions we can easily construct a model for understanding the monetary system we create. We can then apply that model to a simulation to understand our economy and potentially predict our economic future at various levels.

If you were creating money and a monetary system for the first time, how much money would you create? What characteristics or metrics of your economy would you use to determine how much money is created? Some good attributes to consider might be population, quantity of resources, minimum possible unit of currency, characteristics of resources (renewable, perishable, multi-use, etc.), health of the population, and infrastructure of the community. This is of course not an exhaustive list, but this will get us started. Also, as a society continues to improve quality of life and grow in population, it will be necessary to consider how, and when to increase the money supply.

It is difficult to construct a theory of everything in economics, but it is feasible to account for everything in an economy. If every dollar can be accounted for in an economy from year to year, then it is possible to understand the flow of money through an economy. Furthermore, if it is possible to understand the flow of money through an economy, then it is possible to predict the economic future to some extent. We know how many people are in each sector. We know how many people are unemployed. We know the tax rates of individuals and organizations. We know the government budget. We know generally how much people give, spend, and save from year-to-year. We can predict job and salary growth. We can predict when individuals will retire. We can predict when people will jump tax brackets. What we cannot predict (with precision and accuracy) is when individuals and organizations will go into debt or spend their savings. The inability to predict when savings will be spent or debt will be taken on creates a huge problem for predicting the economic future.

We want to predict our economic future for the same reason we want to predict the future in the natural sciences. We want to avoid or mitigate disaster and tragedy. If an asteroid is headed for Earth, we want to know about it and we want to send Bruce Willis up into space to stop it. Likewise, if we could've predicted the stock market crash of 1929, we might've been able to prevent it. Furthermore, this presents perhaps the most compelling reason for economics and the natural sciences to be studied in concert with each other. If economies are rooted in the resource wealth of a country or region, and we are affecting the natural system that supports those resources, then it might be beneficial to consider the economic uncertainty created by the mistreatment of the environment.

Predicting our long term economic future might seem out of reach given the seemingly infinite number of variables that we would need to consider. However, the exercise of trying to predict our economic future isn't for the purposes of knowing exactly what is going to happen. Rather the purpose of the exercise is to know what might happen, how it could happen, and what signals we could find to know that we are heading in the right direction. Of course we can't know with 100% certainty that in 20 years there will be a major economic collapse. But, we can predict the flow of money to some extent. We can predict to some extent the amount of income inequality. We can predict to some extent food production, water scarcity, cost of electricity, and population demographics. And, if we can couple that predictive capability with an understanding of how money can be used to correct issues related to poverty, infrastructure deterioration, environmental quality, and health, then we can begin to optimize the money supply and create the right conditions for steady uninterrupted economic growth.

The first step in attempting to predict our long-term economic future is to understand where every dollar in the economy is today and where it will be one year from now. This miniature exercise would allow us to develop rules about the dynamics of money as it flows through the economy that we can then apply to our system for longer-term simulations. For the purposes of illustration, we can use a small isolated town or a scaled population to help us figure out what we need to capture in order to increase our predictive capability.

Imagine a population of ten people. Half male, half female. Three work for corporations. Three work for the government. Three work for nonprofits. And, one doesn't work. At T_0, the system is set up so that everyone has the same amount of money. In time period 1, T_1, individuals spend, save, give, and get taxed. So, every individual has a spend rate, a save rate, a give rate, and a tax rate. Likewise, every sector has a spend rate, a save rate, a give rate, and a tax rate. So, in this simple example, we can predict where the dollars will end up at the end of T_1. This is assuming we know the spend, save, give, and tax rates of every individual and organization. This is a nice little model.

We can then start to add in things like job growth. So, maybe 1 out of 3 individuals is a manager and gets paid a little bit more than the average, 1 out of 3 is an entry level worker and gets paid less than the average, and 1 out of 3 gets paid the average. We can extrapolate these simple dynamics over 10 or 20 years and see how long it takes before the system breaks. What we find is that the effective money supply shrinks very quickly. And, there is simply no way to stop it from happening. The money supply is actually not changing. Money is flowing into the savings accounts of individuals and organizations to be used in a future time period. Also, more money is flowing to the managers than the entry-level workforce. This, again, is natural, but we need to recognize that it is happening. In a society with a capitalist operating system, income inequality and poverty will grow naturally when the money supply remains constant. So, is a capitalist operating system really a good idea? Yes.

Capitalism as an operating system works better than any other operating system humans have come up with. It works, because it naturally incentivizes the creativity and development of individuals. In combination with a just and compassionate government, capitalism can work for everyone. But it hasn't yet. In our quick simulation of a ten-person economy, we found that the effective money supply is depleted very quickly. We can see how this happens. We are essentially observing the half-life of our money supply. Unlike in pharmacologic, physiologic, or radiologic activity, where we want something to deplete or breakdown quickly, in monetary activity we don't want a half-life that happens quickly. We want our money supply to have a very slow half-life.

We can create a very slow monetary half-life by increasing propensity to give, optimizing tax rates, decreasing debt, inducing more short-term investments, and increasing the velocity of money. Encouraging any of these methods would help to sustain the effective money supply. And, increasing the money supply would effectively make these initiatives possible.

A child-like sense of wonder.

"Economics is a subject profoundly conducive to cliche, resonant with boredom. On few topics is an American audience so practiced in turning off its ears and minds. And none can say that the response is ill advised."

- John Kenneth Galbraith

This document is the second short exploration of a young economist in search of targeted economic solutions to very large global challenges. This discussion has the potential to be very boring, especially to those that are not interested in economics and public policy. However, this discussion also has the potential to be fun and engaging. The study of economics can be as creative as the study of art and design and engineering. We should approach this exploration of economics with a child-like sense of wonder.

Loaves and Fishes

This is not
the age of information.

This is NOT
the age of information.

Forget the news,
and the radio,
and the blurred screen.

This is the time
of loaves
and fishes.

*People are hungry
and one good word is bread
for a thousand.*

-- David Whyte

www.ingramcontent.com/pod-product-compliance
Lightning Source LLC
Chambersburg PA
CBHW070929180526
45168CB00005B/2208